The $UCCESS

MINDSET for

MUSIC PRODUCTION

HOW TO BECOME A SUCCESSFUL MUSIC PRODUCER OVERNIGHT
BY SIMPLY CHANGING YOUR THINKING HABITS

BY CEP FROM SCREECH HOUSE

ISBN-13: 978-1077767492

ISBN-10: 1077767498

PREFACE

Let's get real for a moment. For how long have you been making music? One month? One year? Ten years? Yet, are you still a mediocre home hobbyist or are you already an aspired top-notch artist? You see, there's a high chance you're still failing to produce professional results. You may lack the winning mentality and that ruins your chances of success. Why? Because you may secretly be scared to death to fulfill your highest potential. That's right; your fears are likely to be the ultimate cause for your adversity.

As all humans do, you have fears deep inside, which form limiting beliefs. Your beliefs define whom you are and what you think you are capable of. Unfortunately, they're mere falsities and single-handedly destroy your confidence. You see, while feeling overwhelmed and frustrated, you always get stuck with new challenges. The lack of results thereof quickly drains your patience and kills your motivation. Heavily discouraged you catch yourself thinking, "it's too hard". This losing attitude leads straight to quitting and the easy way out, which exactly confirms what you were already thinking, "I can't do it".

But what would happen if today, you suddenly decide to do things differently? What if you can change something and immediately get the ability to break through limitations. Finally access your untapped potential.

Surprisingly, you can. Because that "something" is you. You are 100% responsible for your current situation, whether you like it or not. Luckily, it's within your control to change it. You can change it easily by shifting your mindset. Hereby, it's absolutely critical to ditch the failure mindset and adopt the success mindset. By obtaining the success mindset and thereby overcoming your limiting beliefs, you too will effortlessly attract successes allover. Your music will improve, your growth will accelerate and your life will become easier overnight. By simply changing your thinking habits, you will become a different person. When you are a different person, you will produce different results. Extraordinary results.

Consequently, you have to destroy your mental barriers and learn how successful people think. That's why this book, *The Success Mindset for Music Production*, dives into the deepest parts of your consciousness and exposes your biggest weaknesses that prevent you from producing outstanding results. Once you understand what's holding you back, you have the personal power to change it immediately. Thereby, you will get many valuable strategies and mind-tricks to help you achieve life-long success. You will finally be able to live up to your highest potential and perform at your all-time best.

WARNING: the information herein is unusual. You will be exposed to mind-bending content that may challenge your beliefs and understandings. We will look at the darkest places of your soul, but also at the brightest areas of your character. If confronting truths make you feel uncomfortable, this book may not be for you. However, if you're ready to challenge your beliefs, this book will offer you the deepest insights about constant failure and lasting success. My mission: to share my knowledge about what it takes to be at your all-time best and stay at your all-time best. Whether you're a music producer or not, it will benefit you in all areas, including your music-making endeavors. You will get to see a bigger picture that reveals the root of bad luck, the root of good luck and eye-opening life lessons.

Now, before we jump in, let me first introduce myself. My nickname is Cep and for many years, I've walked the path of becoming a professional EDM producer. However, I decided to stop chasing a career and instead focusing on sharing my experience with the world. Which partly, you are being exposed to right now.

Furthermore, I am an international author and the creator of *Screech House*. *Screech House* is a well-known platform for ambitious EDM producers who want to learn everything about song-building and sound design. If you also want to discover the lessons, books and courses *Screech House* has to offer, why don't you just pay a visit? Simply click the links below to browse my website, watch my videos or read my books. I'm positive that you will find many missing pieces for your music-making puzzle.

Website: https://screechhouse.com
YouTube: https://youtube.com/screechhouse
Books: https://amazon.com/author/screechhouse

When you find your way to *Screech House*, don't hesitate to drop a comment and subscribe to stay in touch. It's always a pleasure to connect with like-minded readers and producers. Moreover, you can also become a member of my email list by downloading my free hardstyle sample pack via the link below.

Free sample pack: https://eepurl.com/cYAah1

Let the new samples be extremely helpful, but for now, let's focus on this book. Before you start, please be aware of two things.

First, kindly note that my native language is not English, but Dutch. I was born and raised in the Netherlands. So, please forgive me if you come across a few grammatical errors or funny sentence structures. Nonetheless, whether English is your first language or not, you will understand everything just fine.

Secondly, results are always in your own hands and therefore cannot be guaranteed. If you don't intent to change, nothing will happen. Period. This is true for every book you read, every course you take or every advice you follow. Success originates from your freewill choice and willingness to achieve it. It never comes from somebody else. Consequently, I can show you the door, but you have to walk through it.

Nevertheless, you do have the ability to create your own guaranteed results. Therefore, I highly encourage you to implement what you're about to read. Take it seriously, if you are sincere about your future fortune. Just use everything to you advantage and be prepared for a truthful journey that explores the deepest parts of your soul. Buckle up!

ACKNOWLEDGEMENT

All authors want to thank their loved ones and show their appreciation in the acknowledgement section. Despite their good intentions, they sometimes forget the most important person. In fact, this person is the only reason their books have a right to exist. Who is this person, you ask? It's you, the reader.

You see, readers are the only ones who can determine the value of a book. What is a book without a reader? What is an author without a reader? What is the purpose of writing a book without anyone to read the content? What's the point of sharing a message if no one listens?

Of course, I could go ahead and brag about all the awesome people on my *Screech House* channel. I could also pump rainbows into the behinds of my family members. Moreover, I could mention every mentor that has contributed to my skillset today. However, that's not what I'm going to do. Although I very much appreciate them all, they don't mean anything to you, the reader.

That's why I want to dedicate the acknowledgement section exclusively to you. You are the reader of my book. Therefore, it has a purpose and a right to exist. You allow me to take you on a truthful, yet mind-bending ride. Sincerely, thank you.

CONTENTS

INTRODUCTION

To become successful as a music producer, or in any other area of your life, it's crucial to adopt a certain mental attitude. Your attitude is the single most important factor that determines what your future will look like. On the one hand, it can create a prosperous time full of successes and breakthroughs. On the other hand, it can also create a struggling period full of failures and lack of progress. Obviously, you want to avoid the latter at all costs and massively benefit from the former.

So, why is it that our attitudes have such a big impact on our experiences and results? Moreover, what does a successful attitude look like and how can we obtain it?

These are only a few of the many questions this book will answer. Thereby, we will dive into a few essential topics and discover the major problems many of us struggle with that hold us back. Additionally, we will explore how successful people think and expose their hidden mental strategies. This allows you to see the powerful effects of an unproductive negative mindset versus a productive positive mindset. By obtaining the productive positive mindset yourself, your work will rapidly increase in quality and your chances of success will shoot through the roof.

To help you achieve that, we will purposefully start with goal setting in chapter 1. Having a goal or having a bigger purpose defines what success means for you. Furthermore, it dictates what you need to focus on to make it a reality. To make your goal a reality, you also have to stay motivated. Clearly, if your motivation drops, you will lose your desire to work and never reach your destination. That's why in chapter 2, we will dive into our hidden motives and discover what drives us to do something well. Yet, it's not just the "doing" that matters. You also have to guide the "doing" along a path to victory. As you will learn in chapter 3, you can put in all the effort in the world, but in the end still be hopelessly unproductive. Therefore, it's crucial to stay on track, which is easy when you adopt the mindset for success. That's why finally in chapter 4, you will find out how to change your mindset that sets you up for life-long prosperity.

Sounds good? Then let's begin!

CHAPTER 1:

THE PURPOSE OF SUCCESS

Let me ask you something. What exactly is your goal as a producer and what is the objective with your music? Do you have a clear outcome in mind? Can you honestly answer these simple, yet fundamental questions? If you can't or if you're not really sure, you're definitely not alone. It's often hard for us to get our minds clear and see our own (hidden) motives and desires.

The lack of clarity about our goals is one of the major problems many of us struggle with. If you're not sure about what you want, it's hard to focus your actions to reach a destination. This has to do with your "care level". If you don't care enough about reaching your goal, it's practically impossible to stick with your tasks and put in the effort to succeed. After all, you don't have a serious mission to begin with. So, why would you? There's no pressure to do what's necessary to succeed.

However, if your mission is completely clear, you are willing to work towards it until you're victorious. It simply moves you into action, focusing on the tasks at hand. Naturally, it keeps you concentrated on your outcome, which drives the progress. Over time, the progress compounds into impressive results and strengthens your learning experience.

WHY GOALS ARE NOT ACHIEVED

So, why is it that we're having a hard time setting definite goals? Where does it come from and how do accomplished individuals deal with this?

Subconsciously, the absence of having a clear goal often comes from a lack of confidence and trust in our own capabilities. Therefore, we're inclined to take a safe approach. The safe approach is a strategy to protect ourselves from getting hurt. You see, once you set a serious goal, fear kicks in. You suddenly have to be responsible and produce results that you're not yet capable of, which may lead to the scary thought of failure. Of course, nobody likes to fail and experience the humiliating feelings that comes with it.

Furthermore, you may worry that you will lose your face if you can't achieve what you set out to do. Nobody wants to be seen as a loser. Therefore, you keep the act up by saying something along the lines of "it's just a hobby" or "we'll see what the future brings". Nevertheless, in reality, it's simply the fear of being incompetent or being judged that holds you back.

Clearly, no one wants to be confronted with the truth he or she is not good enough. So, we take the safe road. We set vague mediocre goals and adopt limiting beliefs. We easily give up, avoid obstacles and get distracted or frustrated. Eventually, we become lazy, bored and generate depressing self-defeating thoughts. We use the words "try" or "may be" to justify our lack of courage by hiding in the shadow of our own potential.

If we want to step out of our shadow, we have to think differently. We need to change our limiting beliefs and get our acts together to start pursuing our desired goals. A goal is not scary. Ultimately, it's nothing more than a tool.

However, this tool creates the pressure to move us forward. It gives us a sense of direction, responsibility and it challenges our fears. By giving ourselves a serious objective, new possibilities will open and good ideas naturally occur. Why? Because we actually put in the focus and effort to figure out what needs to be done. This will open doors and presents learning opportunities allowing us to reign supreme. Therefore, focusing on a specific outcome is essential for anyone who is committed to bring any task to success.

HOW TO ACHIEVE GOALS

So, how do we have to deal with failure and goalsetting? Moreover, how do successful people deal it? Do they think differently?

First and foremost, realize that failure doesn't exist. It's an illusion that comes from our personal interpretation of an event. To put it simply, it's how we choose to look at a situation. This way, if an event shows that something doesn't seem to work, you have a choice. Do you choose to see it as failure or as a learning opportunity? If you choose to see it as failure, you will experience it as such. You will feel bad about yourself and less motivated to continue. However, if you choose to see it as a learning opportunity, you will also experience it as such. You will be open to the evidence that your method didn't seem to work. Now you can change it. In other words, failure is life giving you a little hint: do it differently next time. "No problem!" you should think. "Let's try something else instead."

That's why, instead of being afraid of failure and risking being confronted with our incompetence, any form of setback is now simply a valuable learning opportunity. As they say, failure leads to success. It shows what doesn't work and that we need to make some changes. Positive changes produce better results. And producing better results is exactly what we're after. That's why failure should be celebrated and not be feared. It merely serves as meaningful feedback, allowing us to grow.

Excellent producers recognize this and use it to grow more quickly. They're simply courageous enough to pursue their goals and stick with them, regardless of what people say. They know it's a (long) process with trial and error. Now, this doesn't mean they like to "fail", but they generally seek the solution within themselves. They are the ones responsible for the results they produce. Moreover, their desire of accomplishment and sense of purpose is strong, because they have faith in their own potential.

This faith gets furtherly enhanced when their goals become part of a bigger purpose. Having a bigger purpose stokes their inner fire, resulting in a better productivity and deeper satisfaction. It's one thing to have positive self-focused goals, but it's another thing to have positive other-focused goals. Having goals that also benefits other people, gives a new dimension of importance and fulfillment. When your work is genuinely about serving others, it will naturally increase in quality and quantity. Why? Because it changes your state of being. You will feel different. It brings a certain hunger for creation and improvement to share value with the world. This gives life more meaning.

On top of that, most successful people have a form of obsession or fascination with their work. They come from a place of strong interest and curiosity. They see the art and potential of being able to reach a certain level of mastery. This drives them to become good at their craft.

You see, making music for example is a form of self-expression. It represents the creation of a human being and shows his/her organizing capabilities. Testing these capabilities and acquiring feedback is essential for self-realization and naturally feels as the right path to take. Moreover, contributing to the self-realization of others even gives a bigger sense of meaning. Inevitably, contribution is a fundamental desire we all share. We all want to be useful and needed. It's a critical feeling screaming to be met that drives us to optimize the state of the entire humanary system.

Thereby, having a target to focus on is essential for directing our actions. This is where goals come in. A goal is not necessarily intended to be reached, but merely serves as a tool to help us become someone else. It puts us on a path for growth. Imagine a goal as a little carrot in front of a bunny on a treadmill. The carrot becomes the motivational trigger for the bunny to start running in that direction. After all, the bunny now has a good reason to move. This way, goals trigger us to do work and to practice our will. They move us forward and help us become better, more valuable. Unescapably, our value will always present itself in everything we set out to do. Therefore, if we are better, our work will be better.

HOW TO OVERCOME THE FEAR OF SUCCESS

But let's get back to where we are stuck: our limiting beliefs. How can we change our limiting beliefs and make sure our work can raise in quality?

Everyone has limiting beliefs in one form or another, which derive from our fears. We all have our struggles and "imperfections". That's why first; you have to accept that. Own it and mean it. It doesn't matter where it came from, right now it's part of who you are and you know it's true. Once you accept and own who you are, you can overcome your fears. The only antidote to fear is courage. This means that you have to face what you're afraid of. Deal with it. You have to make the conscious choice to do what makes you feel uncomfortable. Challenge your character to change your self-image. For example, if setting an ambitious goal makes you feel (a bit) uncomfortable, then you must do it. And "doing it" means committing to it. You should be fully behind your decision and accept whatever comes out. Thereby, the stronger your will and determination, the easier it will be. It's just a matter of intent.

Now, don't see fear as pain or struggle, but as excitement. You're going to do something new that's outside your normal behavior pattern. That's exciting. Adventurous even. It's good to be somewhat nervous and thrilled. Moreover, making a true commitment gives you a sense of power and self-control. It teaches you that you have what it takes to make positive changes. These positive changes will shine through in everything you do, like your music and skills as a producer. Besides, the better results you harvest, the more evidence you collect for the obvious inaccuracy of your limiting beliefs.

So, start with setting simple attainable goals and stick with them until you're successful. Gain some valuable experience. Then set new larger goals, but don't quit. Quitting is the easy way out and leads to mediocrity and poverty. Eventually, when you're getting better, give yourself a purpose bigger than yourself. Literally, assign one to yourself by deliberately choosing for it. See it as your mission or responsibility to contribute to a good cause. This will spark a more powerful type of creativity and commitment. In the end, you will always have to aim at a target to be able to hit it, no matter how big or small.

HOW TO SET GOALS

Now, we understand the importance of having a sense of direction and the role fears play in sabotaging our results. But what does that mean in practice? What do goals look like?

First, truly ask yourself what you want (and not what other people want for you). Do you genuinely want to become a top-notch music producer? Do you only want to have a fun little hobby? Do you desire success? Do you desire a career? Do you feel the need to prove your musical competence to your friends? Do you feel the need to entertain an audience? What is it that you wish to experience? Why do you want to experience that? Do you do it because of fear? Do you do it because you love it? Try to come clear with your own agenda and motives. Clearly, it's crucial to be honest. Listen to how you actually feel and let your heart speak so to speak. There's simply no point in fooling yourself since you'd be the one who suffers.

Once you're crystal clear about your motives and desires, it's time to set your goals accordingly. Ideally, they are exactly in line with your agenda. For example, if you wish to experience being an artist with a number one hit song in the USA, then that should be your aim. After all, it's what you truly want. Of course, a lot needs to happen to realize that desire; so many smaller goals are on that path as well.

Furthermore, a goal needs to be attainable. It needs to be in line with the possibilities. It needs to be in line with the laws of nature and conforms to the constraints of societies. For example, if my goal is to become the queen of England, I should think again. Although there's always a slight possibility, it's not realistic go that route. There are too many reasons why it's not likely to happen. Nevertheless, goals can be bold. Goals can be big. Goals can be out of the box. Our only limitation is our imagination. So, don't hold yourself back by setting mediocre targets. That's just your fear talking you out of greatness. Instead, strive for your biggest dreams. That is, as long as they are realistically possible and attainable. After all, what motivates you more: being a respected number one artist or being an unknown bedroom hobbyist? Exactly. Don't settle for less.

So, figure out what you truly wish to experience. Then, it's time to discover what it takes to get there. Thereby, you can often see the destination, but you have no idea how to reach it. Don't let that discourage you. It's to be expected. A good metaphor I once read that describes this truth is having a nightly trip with your car. The car's headlights project a light-beam that represents everything you can see. You can only see a couple of meters ahead. You don't know what's around the corner or what you come across in the next city blocks. However, by bravely moving towards your destination, new roads and crossing-sections will appear. By making good choices in each moment, you will still find your way home. You just have to keep yourself moving into a defined direction. The act of being in motion automatically takes care of illuminating the entire trip. With the right attitude, you will get yourself moving and you will find a way. Even if that means you occasionally have to turn back to find a different route.

Now, let's take a look at some examples that may give you some ideas what it means to set a goal. Below, you will find eight different goals that may or may not be challenging to adopt. Nevertheless, just use them as examples for your own goalsetting.

> **Goal 1:** I am going to learn my new music software today. I keep working at it until I can make a short song.

- ➤ **Goal 2:** I am going to learn the basics of music theory in the next 2 weeks. I want to make at least 10 melodies that I'm proud of.

- ➤ **Goal 3:** I am going to learn all the settings on my synthesizer to understand what they mean. I will use what I learn and practice until I can make 10 good sounds.

- ➤ **Goal 4:** I have inspiration for making an authentic lead. I am going to apply my ideas immediately and give it my all to produce a nice result.

- ➤ **Goal 5:** For my next project, I will make a trance song with a fast euphoric melody. I already have an idea about the samples and sounds I want to use. I will make sure all instruments work together to produce an awesome track.

- ➤ **Goal 6:** Within the next month, I am going to make the perfect song for my best friend's wedding. I want to make sure all guest have an amazing time.

- ➤ **Goal 7:** I am going to be the best music producer of my generation within 10 years. I will positively influence the lives of millions of people worldwide.

- ➤ **Goal 8:** In 3 years, I have opened an electronic dance music academy in London to teach students the fine art of digital audio production.

HAVE A VISION

Each of these goals give a sense of direction to focus your actions on. However, when you pay close attention, they describe the mindset and not so much the specifics of the outcome. They are centered on what you wish to experience. That's why the mindset should come from a point of vision. A vision is how you see the future and should originate from your desires, which is on a feeling level. You can say that a vision (or dream if you will) is much wider than a goal. It can be a scenario coming true or an outcome being realized.

When the mindset is in such a wider state, the outcome will automatically be optimized, regardless of its shape and form. It will naturally take form as it should be. Furthermore, having a wider scope helps to be more creative. Creativity demands a direction yet can often fare better with an undetermined endpoint. If a result must be a certain way, it's barely impossible to get it that way. That's why in most cases, the more rules you set upon creativity, the less creative the product will be. So, allow your creativity to enfold the outcome for you. As long as your mindset is in check, you will end up with your best work yet.

Most importantly though, when you set goals, it's absolutely critical to give it your all. Any form of doubt or lack of commitment will set you up to fail. Your will to succeed has to come from a feeling space, not so much the intellectual space. How you feel about yourself determines your results. So, make serious goals based on a wider vision, commit and focus your effort towards it. Be positively obsessed, passionate and fascinated with your work. Envision the future and start to live it. Thereby, always think highly of yourself. Be it to become it. It's only a matter of time.

Detach from your ego

Be careful. Don't make the mistake to attach yourself to a particular outcome. Stop thinking the result must be a certain way. That instantly shuts down any other positive results that are different than you expect. Simply don't let your ego get into the way. Keep an open mind and let the process take you wherever it takes you. Surrender to it and allow your creativity to explore new areas. Deal with challenges the best you can. Just drive forward with your goal and everything will naturally fall into place. It will all work out.

For example, if your goal is to go to the moon, it doesn't really matter what your rocket looks like or how it's build. The only things that matters is that it works, that you safely reach the moon and that you (and others) are pleased with the experience. The rocket will be valued by its usefulness, helpfulness and meaningfulness.

In the end, you simply can't predetermine every step in the way to force a specific outcome. Look at what works and what doesn't. Look at what is appreciated and what isn't. Then simply adjust accordingly. It's not rocket science. The same goes with dating. You'd love to experience her company, but if she says "no", hey, that's fine too. Accept it and move on. Find someone else who actually appreciates your presence.

Illustratively, I quite often get questions from people asking me how to make a sound like this or that. They try to recreate certain sounds from their favorite artists, exactly as they do. The problem is that they want the outcome to be a specific way, which kills the creativity and options for it to be different. Furthermore, it's merely impossible to recreate a particular sound without knowing all the exact instruments and effects being used.

Instead, we have to flip the mindset by a full 180 degrees. Of course, it's good to be inspired by others and learn from their methods, but we shouldn't take everything too literally. We also have to find our own ways. That's why, try to be open with your approach, but strive to do it good. Have a vision in mind what you want to achieve, but don't try to pin down every little step. Don't force things to be, but allow things to become. Moreover, allow yourself to grow. Once you come from that place of allowance, you will see that you're much more flexible and creative. Your results will be much better and your productivity will increase.

Now, will the results match the sounds of your favorite artist? May be not completely. But do they work? Yes. Do they sound good? Yes. Do people appreciate them? Most likely, yes. Most importantly, your creations will be original and authentic. They are exactly how they should be. And when you share them with others, they may start asking you: "How did you make that sound?" and "How can I recreate it?" Then you think and say, "Whatever comes out is how it should be."

By the way, if you desire to make professional sounds yourself, you can easily gain the expertise by reading the Sound Design for Beginners guide. In this detailed guide, I will take you along every essential setting on a basic synthesizer. This way, you will understand exactly what each setting does, how to use it and most importantly, why to use it. If you think you can benefit from that, just visit this link to get started: https://www.amazon.com/dp/B07MCQLNLJ

THE IMPORTANCE OF PURPOSE

To capture the essence of this chapter, let me share a little story. Back in the day, we're talking early 2000s; I often played around in my newly favorite D.A.W (Digital Audio Workstation): FL Studio. By the way, if you're an FL Studio beginner yourself, you can now get my top-selling title, the FL Studio

Beginner's Guide, by visiting this link: https://www.amazon.com/dp/B07D8JM9W9. Anyhow, without a clear mission, I was hardly able to make decent sounds, melodies or even songs. I didn't really know what I was doing, because my level of understanding was too low. Admittedly, I also didn't give it my all to learn it seriously. I tried of course, and at least I was able to create a couple of low quality snippets. All in all, very amateurish material to the well-trained ears.

Then one day, a good friend of mine had an interesting idea. He let me listen to a high-energy rock song and asked me to make an EDM version of it. "Interesting", I thought. After a few seconds of thinking time I said, "Let's give it a shot!" And there I went, pursuing a bigger goal for the first time in my music-making life.

Surprisingly, while I started working on the remix, my energy was different from normal. It was positive, creative and my results were getting better than ever. This gave me extra motivation and a sense of purpose. I started to believe in myself and focused on a positive outcome. After all, I felt the responsibility to serve my friend. I thought, "I want to make this song as good as I can and proudly present it to my friend". That though was my mission and drove me towards something good. I couldn't see it yet, but it felt right. So, I continued.

Finally, after a few days of dedication, the last elements had been arranged and the track was officially finished. "Wow, this is really good", I realized. I felt proud and satisfied. Then, I sent a copy to my friend and excitingly waited for his reply. Just as me, he was also very impressed and more than pleased with the result. "Where did that all come from?" I asked myself. Not knowing yet that my mindset and sense of purpose were crucial for my experience.

A few months later, I chatted with an acquaintance. He suggested sending my remix to a professional records label. I decided to give it a go and curiously waited for a response. A while after, I received an email from the company. They wanted me to send them a finalized version of the track, because they would like to release it. I was thrilled and couldn't believe it. "Was my song actually good enough for a release? That's amazing!"

Now, I never actually sent back a finalized version. I felt it was only a one-time shot and I wasn't ready yet to live up to that quality standard. Of course, looking back right now, the song was far from being perfect. Nevertheless, at the time, it was absolutely my best work I was capable of achieving.

This just goes to show that having a clear mission with a positive open mindset is crucial for getting your best results. Your best results may still be far off from your ultimate goal right now, but when you keep focusing on your outcome with the right intent, you automatically do what's most optimal for your gains and growth. After all, your growth improves your qualities. Your qualities dictate your success.

Want to have success? Challenge yourself. Give yourself a serious purpose and work towards it with a positive mind. Want it bad enough to stick with it for the long run. Thereby, don't let your fears talk you down and have the courage to do it anyways. Then, let life surprise you. And when you've had your fun, you've had your success, set out a new mission. Keep embarking on new journeys to experience everything you wish to do.

CHAPTER 2:

THE MOTIVATION FOR SUCCESS

Even if you're the most ambitious positive person on the planet, you're still human. Humans are not robots. We have our current limitations, capabilities and emotional states. This means that our willpower, energy and focus will vary from time to time. Furthermore, we sometimes have phases that our inspiration, motivation and self-belief take a hit. Eventually, this compromises our progress. Less progress means less results and less growth. In other words, our motivation is quite critical for achieving success.

WHAT IS MOTIVATION?

Now, what exactly is motivation and where does it come from?

To put it simply, our motivation is the positive feeling we get when we trust and believe in a desired outcome. This spikes our creativity, inspiration and energy. It leads to good ideas, promotes a clear focus and decisiveness. It gives us a sense of hunger or lust to put in the work to achieve a result, even if we don't know exactly how to get there. Our motivation is our inner fire, inner believe and inner trust that drives us to produce something valuable or meaningful. Of course, value and meaning are personal things. Hence, everyone's motivation is different. It's always based on our own reason and value system. After all, it comes from our personal emotions. E-motion: energy in motion. The driving force that makes things happen (or not).

WHY DOES MOTIVATION COME AND GO

So, why does our motivation sometimes take a hit? Why can't we have a stable stream of inspiration and a steady rate of productivity?

Motivation comes from a feeling space. It originates from our desires and beliefs of experiencing that. If we genuinely keep believing in obtaining a desired outcome, our motivation will get a boost. However, if we stop doing that and poor in some negative self-talk, our motivation will gradually fade away. You see, it's all about trust and faith. Do you truly have the trust in your capabilities of achieving a particular result? Do you honestly have faith in accomplishing your mission? If you do, you don't need to read this book, because you're already fired up. But if you don't, you may want to continue reading.

The problem is that most people lack a deeper sense of trust and believe in their capabilities to attain that incredible outcome. We don't have enough faith in our own potential. Although we might act as if, deep from the inside we have doubts. We secretly question our competence. We sometimes look for excuses why we can't have something. We also find strategies to talk ourselves out of success. Unfortunately, we will actually be successful in doing that. And by doing that, our motivation will shrink away until there's nothing left other than a depleted longing soul.

It's important to understand that these doubts and destructive thoughts come from our fears. In fact, all negative emotions derive from our fears.

Fears make us feel vulnerable and steal from our potential. They suck away our motivation and induce low quality thoughts and feelings, like hate, anger, greed, guilt, anxiety, shame, grief, frustration, doubt, annoyance, despair, jealousy, panic, loneliness, worthiness, etc. Unfortunately, we often deal with our fears by shoving them under the rug and developing attitudinal strategies to protect ourselves. Thereby, we become more self-centered, needy and take things more personally. However, these are just shallow acts, facades or cover-ups in a desperate attempt to hide a painful truth: we feel scared, vulnerable and weak from the inside. Ultimately, fears are self-created and part of whom we are. Since we all have them in one form or another, we all experience motivational problems from time to time. Of course, everyone in their own way.

Fears let us do things for the wrong reasons or values. By believing they're true, we trap ourselves into thinking that our ideas are in our best interest. Nevertheless, when we let fear take over, we may attain some short-term benefits, but in the long term, we will always have to deal with harmful or destructive consequences. For example, if you fear not being appreciated, you may undertake ventures in which you seek recognition. Seeking recognition then becomes your internal motivation. It drives the reasons for your venture. However, the search for recognition is all about you. You only do a certain task for selfish reasons. Yet, there's nothing "out there" that will ever satisfy your thirst for recognition. Hence, you're chasing a lie. No matter how much recognition you'll get, it will never be enough. After all, you haven't outgrown the fear yet, thus you will constantly feel the need to make up for that problem you have inside.

That's why in the long run this will never work. It will drain your energy and doesn't give the fulfillment you forcefully hoped to gain. Therefore, chasing a fear-based mission will be nothing more than a shallow experience full of conflict, struggles and frustration. Why? Because fear is the sum of our negative feelings. Feeding into it enhances their presence. Over time, they will grow and overpower our minds. In the process, you slowly lose drive, motivation and inspiration. Your life becomes darker, more draining and tiring. It is at that time depression kicks in to scream: "Wake up! It's time to change."

HOW TO STAY MOTIVATED FOREVER

Obviously, this is not the optimal route. So, how do we optimize our motivation? How can we stay inspired and keep trust in our own capabilities to produce a good outcome?

When you understand that fears are at the core of our motivational problems, you can see the solution. We simply don't have to live by our fears. We're in charge. We have the power to make different choices. That means we can choose to change ourselves. All it takes is a focused intent to introduce a different mindset.

Instead of having fear-based reasons that come from a negative feeling space, we should adopt love-based reasons. Don't let the word "love" scare you. This is not a hippie movement, rather a powerful concept to understand. Love is about other, what you can give. Not about self, what you can get, like fear. It's about genuinely giving, sharing, caring, trusting, believing, helping, supporting, understanding, etc. Thereby, love-based reasons are productive, constructive and creative. They come from a positive feeling space. For example, having a true desire to make an awesome song for your audience (focusing on giving), gives a completely different energy than when your desire comes from the idea of impressing your friends to get their approval (focusing on getting). In the former, you will experience a clear high-energy stable vibe. In the latter, you will experience an unclear and unstable vibe, including subtle negative feelings, like mild anxiety, elevated stress levels or doubts. If you're like most people out of whack with these signals, they're pushed away in the subconscious mind. However, when you start to pay close attention to how you feel, you will learn your exact motives in the blink of an eye.

You see, it's all about your motive. Your motive becomes your motivation. So, question your motives. Do you do it because of fear or love? What are your reasons? What are your values? Why are you doing what you are doing? Is there something you need to prove? Is there something you genuinely wish to share? Do you do it just for you? Do you do it to serve a bigger purpose? Dive in and be honest about it. Thereby, don't let your motives scare you. The truth of the matter is that most things we undertake are fear-driven. That's just who we currently are. It's up to us to outgrow it.

Now, this doesn't mean you can't get results with fear-based motives. Quite in the contrary. You can use them to fuel anything you wish to accomplish. In fact, many people have accomplished incredible feats of mastership this way. They start by convincing themselves that they want something bad enough. Thereby, they put in the work, they hustle and grind until they're "successful". However, when they finally have it, they slowly start to realize that their experience is not what they expected. Although it can give a quick ego boost in the beginning, soon after, they're left with feelings of emptiness and shallowness. After all, their accomplishment didn't solve that fear problem they have inside. They only tried to make up for how they really felt, which of course, can never work.

Some people will come to this realization and decide to change how they feel about themselves. However, other people don't. Ignorantly, their ego gets in the way and they think they need to work more, grind more and hustle more to become happy and fulfilled eventually. So, off they go, chasing another lie in a never-ending attempt to compensate for how they actually feel inside. Nonetheless, the years or decades of grinding will suck the lives out of them and consequently they end up as lone, grumpy and miserable persons.

That's why the long-term effects of any fear-focused venture is self-defeating and possibly even harmful to others. You simply can't keep up with your own lies forever. It starts to consume your mind and steal your happiness. What's the point of having success, if you feel awful? Can we even call that "success" in the first place? Eventually, the effects of your efforts will always show themselves. It's up to you to decide if you like the consequences. If you don't, maybe that's a sign you have embarked on a journey with fear-based motives.

It simply doesn't have to be this way. Why choose a route full of struggles, frustrations, unhappiness, pain and negativity to get where you want to be? With only a shift in mindset, you can just as well have happiness, fulfillment, joy and positivity in that process. Moreover, it will get you there faster and easier as everything will fall into place more smoothly. Now, which route sounds better to you?

In the end, your work will only become a grind or hustle when you do it out of fear. You feel like you "have to" do it, because you're doing it for the wrong reasons. On the contrary, your work becomes a joyful game or challenge when you do it out of love. You feel like you "want to" do it, because you're doing it for the right reasons. So, it's just a matter of choosing which feeling space to come from. If you choose correctly, you will be rewarded with high levels of motivation and desire.

HOW TO MOTIVATE YOURSELF

So, how do we change our mindset and how should we think? What are some practical approaches to improve our motivation, inspiration and trust?

Obviously, we want to stay motivated and have a fun experience with our music-making endeavor. Therefore, all it takes is a change in our beliefs. By changing our beliefs, we can control how we feel. Now, instead of the word "belief", we can use the word "conviction". Conviction comes from a deeper place of ourselves and shows more determination. It's an internal power of will that moves you forward with confidence and certainty. By shifting your mind to a place of positive conviction, it becomes absolutely clear that the outcome will be realized. It removes any doubts and uncertainty about reaching your goal. It's definitive, because you choose to think that way. You will reach your destination, no questions asked.

For instance, what motivates you to get out of bed in the morning to make breakfast? Of course, the positive experience that it will bring. Although it hasn't happened yet, you simply forecast a beneficial event in which you gain. You are convinced that you're going to get a rewarding feeling, thus you're willing to take action. By this straightforward everyday example, you can immediately see the power of a convinced mind. By convincingly picturing a positive result, your motivation rapidly increases. If you do this for everything you set out to do, you will never run without.

Again, this type of strong conviction mostly has to come from a feeling space. You have to be fully committed to attain what you desire. Else, it's just another lie you're telling yourself to escape the truth: you're afraid. It's easier to hide and stay comfortable than to step out of your comfort zone and express all the potential you have inside.

Practically, this means you have to move forward with your purpose and convince yourself that you will get there. Step up and take responsibility. It comes down to a mental attitude. Practice the attitude of conviction and belief. Create certainty with your mind, even when it's unclear in reality. Keep at it consciously from an intuitive level. This will boost your motivation and inspiration. Have trust and faith in a positive outcome and come from a place of knowing. Know that you are capable, even if you haven't done it yet. Know that you will get there, even if you haven't been there yet. Know that you have it in you to be whoever you need to be. Envision your goal being realized and truly believe you will experience it. Keep envisioning your biggest desire and focus on what you have to do to get there.

Furthermore, try to avoid fear-based reasons. If it feels wrong, it probably is. Ask yourself, if there's a fear attached to what you are doing. If the answer is yes, release that motive. Just drop the act. Have the courage to let it go and find a better motive. There's nothing you have to prove. So, focus on what you love to experience, not on what you fear to experience. Make sure your goals come from love-based reasons. It has to feel right, intuitively. You must do it, because you love it. If you love it, you will automatically develop a passion, fascination and obsession. Naturally, this should drive you effortlessly to a state of flow and productivity. Getting into the zone so to speak. You simply can't stop and don't want to. It will lighten your inner-fire to embark on a new journey with confidence.

By the way, don't pin yourself down by thinking you can only love this or that. The truth is; you're capable of loving anything. It all depends on your openness and willingness to invest your effort into something. For example, if you've never made music in your life, how can you love making music? You have to experience it first to develop a passion for it. That is, if the experience is driven by a positive hands-on attitude. Once you get a feel for the potential benefits of your undertaking, you will naturally start to like it. Ultimately, almost everything has valuable possibilities to offer. It's only a matter of mindset if you're willing to give it a chance.

EXTERNAL FACTORS THAT AFFECT MOTIVATION

Next to our own mindset, are there also other factors that have an effect on our motivational state? And how can we deal with triggers from the outer world?

Now clearly, there are also external factors that can contribute to our motivational state. In particular, our environment and the connections we have with the people around us. We all interact with each other and communicate how we feel, mostly subconsciously. This will tell the story of our intent. However, it can have a big effect on how we make each other feel.

You see, when people genuinely want to be helpful or valuable, you will pick up these well-known positive vibes. Their intent is to contribute and support the people around them. Sometimes, you will also meet people that send out these negative vibes. Their intent communicates that they're not acting in the best interest of those around them. This way, we all send out signals that affect everyone we come across. Consequently, the people around us can affect how we feel and steal our energy, motivation and confidence. That is, if we let them. These are the toxic persons or energy vampires. On the flipside, there are also the individuals that give us energy, motivation and confidence. They lift us up and make us feel good about ourselves. As they say, you are the average of the five people you spend the most time with. Be careful whom you choose.

That's why it's extremely important to pay attention to the people around you. Are they helpful, supportive and positive? Are they complaining, unsupportive and negative? Which vibes do you get from them? Do they help you on your mission? Who is building you up and who is breaking you down? Find the answers to these questions and come to honest conclusions. Thereby, try to limit the contact with destructive individuals. This sometimes means shying away from life-long friends or family members. Of course, keep the positive people around you and may be spend more time with them. They're the ones who believe in your potential and understand the path you choose to take.

Furthermore, it's a good idea to hang out more with constructive like-minded people. They're growing in a similar direction as you are. You can easily find them in certain groups or online communities. A group or community can have a vision or goal in line with yours. Sharing a vision or common goal strengthens the relationship of all included members. Above all, interacting in a constructive group will slingshot you forward. Everyone is willing to share and guide his/her friends to success. We simply all know different things and have different specialties or talents. We all have something to share and somewhere to grow.

Overall, find your people and don't be afraid to let go of a dysfunctional relationship. Just connect to the ones you resonate with. Embrace the ones who can serve as your sparring-partners. Search for mentors or teachers who can add value to your life. Collaborate. Stay open to new relationships and see if you can share ideas. Look online for communities that already do what you wish to accomplish. Search on forums, websites and social media. Do what's necessary to optimize your social environment.

On the same note, your direct physical environment can also contribute to how you feel. For example, a dark, small 2 by 2 office-cubicle may drain your energy completely, while a light, big-windowed room with nature view may boost your mood. Therefore, just like being selective with your friends, you also have to be selective with your surroundings. Be in places that are nurturing and bring out the best in you. Avoid the places that wear you out. Create your personal positive environment, whatever that means to you. After all, it can mean the difference between victory and defeat.

Likewise, we have to consider our personal well-being as well. The way we take care of ourselves has a big impact on our energy levels, focus and motivational state. Our health and habits dictate how we feel physically and mentally. Factors like sleep, nutrition, bad habits, addictions and health issues all play a role in affecting our mindset. For example, when you decide to skip a night of sleep, how would you feel the day after? Similarly, how would you feel when you consistently eat junk food, smoke cigarettes and sit on the couch every day? Obviously, these habits will sabotage any good intentions you may have. Hence, it's vital to take good care of yourself if you wish to stay on track.

So, review your choices and consider changing the habits that jeopardize your well-being. Does your diet suck? Change it. Do you lack physical exercise? Go to the gym. Do you play videogames the whole day? Stop it. Do you get back pains from you matrass? Buy a new one. Do whatever is necessary to improve your conditions for maximum performance. It's literally that easy. You just have to want to do it. And you will, because you're serious about your mission.

In the end, whether we allow the environment, our friends or our habits affect our motivation; we always have to seek the solution in ourselves. Take responsibility for how you feel and change it. You have that power. Clearly, this doesn't mean you will always have the same amount of energy every day. Some days are more challenging than others are. Nevertheless, as long as you do the best you can, you will get ahead and be satisfied.

So, if you're motivation fades away, let others inspire you. If you're not in the mood, take a walk in nature. If you're too tired, schedule a long night of sleep. Just take the first step forward, and before you know it, you're unstoppable again.

THE POWER OF FAITH

To capture the essence of this chapter, let me share a quick story. As being the author of this book, it's my purpose to bring it to success. I have to keep putting in the work to write the manuscript, without really knowing where it will go. Literally, as I'm typing the words for this paragraph, I still don't know what comes next. This challenges my inspiration and motivation strongly.

Now, I could give into the feeling of uncertainty. I could be doubtful and convince myself it's a bad idea. I could choose to think, "Just stop it. Who cares about your philosophical mumble anyways?" And I have to admit. Sometimes that negative voice start to enter my mind. It carefully tries to negotiate me out of creation with self-defeating thoughts.

Luckily, I know better. I simply shift my focus away from that negative voice and stop feeding into it. I point it towards positivity with strong love-based reasons. I convince myself that the book will be good. It will be valuable and meaningful to every reader at least to some extent. It will contribute to a bigger purpose that enlightens people across the globe. Thereby, I don't care about my personal gain, but what it can do for others. It needs be eye opening, truthful and helpful to you. This deeper belief and focus stokes my motivation. It feels 100% right and there's no more doubt in my mind. It will be a success, also, regardless of what others think. I refuse to question this motive whatsoever.

Now, this still means I don't know where it's literally going. But that's not important. All that is important is my trust and faith in a positive outcome, regardless of its shape and form. Hence, I only know the bigger vision that I desire to experience. My intent is clear and I believe that I can do it. When I can keep that up, everything will naturally fall into place and I will be motivated to finish this task. And since you're reading this now, I have been successful in doing so.

Want to be successful? Have complete trust and faith in your own potential and defeat your negative inner voice. Ditch any negative fear-based motives and convince yourself with positive love-based reasons. Pair that with a strong sense of purpose and you will be unstoppable. It's just a matter of doing it.

Nevertheless, if you're motivation and inspiration still takes a hit, don't panic. Simply calm down and give yourself some time off. Have a break or go away. Refresh yourself and come back recharged to finish what you set out to do. But most importantly, always remember why you're doing it in the first place. If you have the right reasons, your hunger will naturally come back.

Additionally, it can help to try new ways of doing things. Don't get stuck in old routines. Search and implement new ideas. Have some new (exciting) experiences. Experiment with your work. Think outside the box once in a while. If anything, it can only contribute to your growth as a producer and spark your inner fire.

CHAPTER 3:

THE PATH TO SUCCESS

You now have your mission and you're motivated to bring it to a success. But how do you stay on track? How do you know you're implementing the right strategies and follow good advice that lead to your goal? What keeps you on the right path? Obviously, you don't want to end up wasting your time and effort. Therefore, you need to move forward efficiently by taking steps in a fruitful direction.

HOW TO FIND YOUR WAY TO SUCCESS

So, how do we define a fruitful direction and how do we know we're doing the "right" things?

Plot twist! You don't know. But here's the trick... Everything you undertake will automatically fall into place when you move forward with a positive mindset focused on your goal(s) and vision. You see, your motivation to be constructive naturally moves you to doing the right things. Your mind will fill in the blanks and asks the right questions. Questions and ideas will occur to make something happen. For example, if you're committed to the goal of building a house, you naturally start to think, "What type of house do I want to build?" "Where does it need to be located?" "What should it look like?" "What is the blueprint and which materials do I need?" And on and on it goes.

By listening to your thoughts and taking actions on your ideas, you will automatically figure it out. Without second-guessing, you will conduct some research. You will look online for tips and processes. You will contact builders or architects. You will do whatever needs to be done to make it happen. Why? Because you set your mind to it. You just really want to. That deeper inner desire is the driver for success, regardless of how you get there.

It's actually that simple, yet so easy to talk yourself out of. That's why it's more a matter of motivation, conviction and desire than a matter of figuring out the "right path". Don't focus on the "right path". It will take care of itself. Focus on what you truly want and give it your all. Set your mind to something and listen to your thoughts, feelings and inner-voice in the process. Whatever that leads you to, will be the most optimal for your growth. After all, you are always exactly in the right place at the right time.

CARE WHAT YOU WISH FOR

But how should we feel or think to optimize our results? Is there any attitude we can adopt that boosts the qualities of our work?

Your mindset plays a huge factor when it comes down to the quality of your work. You should connect with it, put in your soul and come from a place of caring. When you care, you put yourself in an optimal state to produce the highest quality you're currently capable of. It primes your mind to take it seriously, because you're producing something that is part of who you are. However, at the moment your care-level drops, you will start to slack, bungle and become distracted or impatient. Why? Because you hold yourself back from doing better. Subconsciously, you know you're not giving it your best. Thereby, your creation will suffer and this starts to eat at your conscious. A half-assed creation will provide false evidence for your lack of skill. This can induce fear, like doubts, incompetency and insecurity. After all, you just proved yourself not to be good enough and your work confirms that.

So, by lowering the bar of what you're truly capable of, you can hurt yourself as well as others. You see, if your half-assed creation is to be shared with others, you will not treat them optimally. After all, you have the qualities to give them something better. This is taking the easy way out and it will show. People will notice the lack of quality and pick up that you try to get off easy. In response, they may not appreciate it or feel that it's a waste of time. Just ask yourself; what do you think what would happen when we all treat each other without caring? Alternatively, what do you think what would happen when we all treat each other with full care? What do you think is a more optimal way of living?

Whether we like to admit it or not, our work will always reflect how much we care. The amount of care shows the truth of our love-based and fear-based motives. If we come from a place of love for our work, the results will reflect this higher quality. If we come from a place of fear, our endeavors will automatically show this lower quality, especially in the long run. Thereby, anything fruitful and sustainable originates from love-based motives. Anything unfruitful and unsustainable originates from fear-based motives. That's why, all it takes is a positive mindset to get on the right path. The path is already there. You just have to choose to walk it.

HOW TO STAY ON THE RIGHT PATH

But what does this mean in practice? How do we apply this on a day-to-day basis?

Now in theory, this sounds wonderful, but we also have to look at everyday life. We're still humans and have our difficulties. So, what are some good strategies to stay on the right path? How can we keep our mind focused on producing positive love-based creations, without talking ourselves out of success?

First and foremost, any venture you set your mind to must originate from a place of love. This may sound "hippie" to most people, but it's the truth. Make sure that you always come from a pure constructive intent. This will give you positive energy and a good vibe to create something of true value. Thereby, your actions should be in line with your deeper being. This means having a clear desire from a feeling space to achieve something meaningful. It should come from the core of you. The real you.

For example, when your goal is to make an awesome melody for your song, don't just go through the motions. Don't let it all come from your intellect. Instead, make it an intuitive process and connect your emotions to it. Your emotions will forecast the experience of what your awesome melody should feel like. This feeling is the information you get that you can use to make it awesome indeed. Listen to it. It's a crucial message that you can benefit from. After all, music is emotion.

A good way to engage your feelings is to visualize the experience of your melody being played on a big party or event. You should feel the goosebumps of your own melodic piece. You should experience the joy and pleasure of your epic song. So, when you need to design the next part of your new melody, ask yourself "How should the melody flow so that it makes me feel awesome?" or "How does it sound when it gets me in ultimate ecstasy?" Hear it in your mind. Fill in the progression that brings you to the most positive emotional state. This will render high-quality ideas and fill in the blanks to move your melody to an ultimate state of awesomeness. That's why; always connect deeply with your work, no matter what you're working on. Be personally invested. Make it a positive obsession or passion. This will undoubtedly set you on your path to success.

While we happen to be on this topic and if you'd like to improve the quality of your own melodies, feel free to read The Ultimate Melody Guide. The Ultimate Melody Guide is another book I've written to share the tricks I personally use to create professional melodies quickly. Yes, you do need to know a few bits about music theory, but only on a surface level. So, if you're songs can benefit from more musical intelligence, I encourage you to obtain a copy by visiting this link: https://www.amazon.com/dp/B07F889F5Q. When you're ready, let's continue.

Another strategy to stay on the right path is to be aware that success leaves clues. This means that other people have already accomplished something similar to what you set out to do. They have found a way that works and produce results. By looking at what they did, you can learn so much and easily walk in their footsteps. Walking in other people's footsteps could crush your learning curve and prevent you from making unnecessary mistakes. This way, we can use others for inspiration, motivation and education. By following their lead, they can guide us on a proven road to victory.

HOW TO FIND THE RIGHT MENTOR

So, how do we find these so-called mentors and how do we know if they're any good on our road to victory? Are there any signs we can pick up to understand if their strategies also work for us?

Of course, to walk in someone's footsteps your first need to find a mentor. Good mentors provide you with value to move forward. They can be anyone and come from anywhere. It can be that new person at work. It can be your brother or sister. It can even be that kid across the street. You see, a mentor is just a person that can teach you something you wish to understand. That's why it's important to keep an open mind of what a mentor should be.

That being said, you're goal-orientated. You probably don't have time to find mentors, let alone find the right ones. So, is there a place where you can immediately select your potential teachers? Surprisingly, there is. This place is called the internet. The internet has opened the door to a new level of growth and possibilities. With just a few clicks and thought-out search-terms, you can find people across the globe who provide the answers you're looking for. By simply connecting to their message, you too can learn what they do.

It's really that simple, yet we often slack in this area. Why we tend to slack, we've already discovered. We're not committed enough and we don't always have a focused positive mindset. Because if we do, we naturally consult our favorite search engine and dedicate to finding the solutions we wish find.

For example, if your goal were to make a professional trance kick-drum, would it occur to you to just type in the words: "trance kick tutorial"?

Assuming you're dedicated, of course it would. It's all about your level of seriousness of accomplishing a goal. Are you committed enough, determined enough and convinced enough? Because if you are, you were already doing it. That's why no one needs to tell you what path to take. You already know that you can solve any case with a proactive approach, even if it takes a while. So, be positively committed and you will instinctively do the right things. You will find the right people to learn from and take the actions you need to take. Thereby, your actions will always reflect how strongly you believe in your mission.

Even though new territory is unknown, it is waiting for you to be explored. Therefore, if you can't do something, learn it. If you don't know how, search it. If you think you don't have any talents, convince yourself otherwise. The point is that your willingness and openness to learn is critical to be effective. Allow others to help you. Be a learner, discoverer and experimenter. The solutions are already waiting for you.

Now, if you ever doubt, listen to your inner-voice. Ask yourself questions. "Is this person any good?" "Is this person a scam?" "Does this person help me?" "What is the vibe I get from him or her?" "Do I get advice that works for me?" Understand how you feel about someone. Do you resonate with the message? If you honestly answer these questions, you will know what to do. If it works for you, keep it. If it doesn't, let it go. Follow the right advice and avoid any misguided opinions.

HOW TO KNOW IF SOMEONE IS WORTH YOUR TIME

A good trick you can use to see if someone knows what he or she is talking about is to look for simplicity. Usually (not always), simplicity and elegance are key. If something is too complicated, it's typically not fundamental, thus the teachings could be bloated, distorted and full of fluff. Thereby, the amount of "beating around the bush" often indicates a weak sign of success. Let me give you an example.

Sometimes, I come across tutorials where people teach how to make fat leads. They use extreme settings, a ton of effects, along with a 30-minute rant of the importance of their method. However, when they show the results at the end, their leads still sounds underwhelming, especially compared to professional artists. Obviously, even if they have good intentions, their methods are somewhat flawed. They don't know exactly how to reach that level of quality. Of course, that's okay, but why would I continue to connect with their teachings? I've already examined their work as not being fundamental. It's not simple enough and not elegant enough. That's why I have to make a conscious choice to move on and may be find a better teacher to learn from.

Another cue you can use to see if someone is worth your time, is to look at his or her perspectives. Perspectives are key. There are a gazillion ways of getting results and not one single set-in-stone method. So, if a teacher claims to have the only solution, the absolute method or the one-and-only strategy, it's probably flawed or incomplete. In reality, results depend on contexts, variables, and the limits of our imagination and creativity. That's why the words to look for is: "it depends".

As a final tip, pay more attention to what people do and less to what they say. The doing produces the results, not the saying. When their doing is different from their saying, it's a contradiction or inconsistency. This can indicate falsities or incomplete information. Hence, always question if they live by what they preach. Thereby, only listen to their words if they're in line with their actions.

This way, looking for inconsistencies, perspectives and simplicity will keep you on the right path. That is, as far as mentors and teachings go. Connect that to your own common sense and you will naturally have a gut feeling of what's helpful and what's not. The real question is; do you choose to follow it?

How to find what works for you

Other than that, just look at what successful people are doing and model their work. Understand what they are doing, fundamentally. Then, find your own ways to implement that new understanding. Develop your own strategies tailored to your goals and realize that we all have a different route to take. Thereby, you don't want to reinvent the wheel. If something is proven to work, why change it? That is, unless you can improve upon it.

So, it doesn't matter where and in which way you gather information. Find what works for you and learn from the best. As a music producer for example, you can study the work of masters and pay close attention to the songs you like. Reverse engineer their sounds, instruments, arrangements and compositions. Listen to their qualities. Analyze each song for harmonics, frequencies and stereo imagery. Learn the relationships and balance between the existing elements. Put in the effort and do what's necessary to understand what it takes to create a professional track. Examples abound, all available for you to dissect. The recipe is already out there. It's up to you to discover it. You can either proactively dive in and start your journey or passively wait on the sideline and settle for mediocrity. And it goes without saying that if you were fully committed; you'd already be on your way.

In the end, you have to make your own choices. No one other than you decides what to do, where to go, and how to do it. Therefore, the only way to stay on track is to build it yourself. That's why, focus on your vision, your purpose, your goal, and keep defining what to do next. Describe what your current problem or sticking point is and find out what you can do right now to solve it. Keep making better choices, step by step, towards your desired outcome. Do this consistently and there's no other possibility than achieving success.

HOW TO AVOID FAILURE

Nonetheless, are there also some common mistakes we make that let us go off track? What are some issues that hold us back and how can we fix that?

One of the things that hold us back is that we often think we literary need to plan each step ahead. We want to work out every detail before we feel safe to move forward. However, it kills our progress. It leads to procrastination and postponing what we desire. There's simply always more to discover. Therefore, don't fall into trap of convincing yourself you still need more information. Likewise, don't fall for the idea that now is not the right time. It's never the "right" time. In other words, stop any paralysis by analysis and do what you have to do.

You see, the need for this perfect preparation can come from the fear of the unknown and the fear of being inadequate. The fear generates self-doubts. It moves you in a direction where you think you need to obtain every relevant skill possible before you can start doing what you actually want. For example, if you really want to make a techno song, why would you keep spending your time on overanalyzing, overthinking or over-preparing how your music-making software works? Why don't you just start with the basics, jump right in and try to make some songs? See what obstacles come up and just try to overcome them. Don't try to predict or anticipate on all possible problems. That's an endless story. Let there first be one before you try to fix it. Once a problem shows itself, you can then fix it by becoming a better version of yourself. One who knows how to deal with it. After all, a problem only points out what you need to learn. After that, it doesn't exist anymore.

Naturally, if you just start doing what you are supposed to be doing, you will learn along the way. On the fly so to speak. You will learn exactly what you need to learn. The problems you need to solve to get to your goal will present themselves organically. They will perfectly reflect in which areas you need to grow. So, don't hold yourself back, have some courage and just dive into the deep. Let the process of evolution do its job and keep building upon what you know and what you have. This allows you to learn first-hand in practice, without having to beat around the bush.

Another thing that can hold us back is that we mistakenly think our efforts are always useful. We feel good about our busyness during the day without realizing it doesn't get us closer to our goals. This is busyness for the sake of busyness. Doing for the sake of doing. Life is not about busyness or doing. You can be busy the whole day counting butterflies, but it doesn't help you get any closer to fulfilling your mission. Moreover, how is it helpful or valuable for others?

Usually, this fake type of busyness originates from a lack of motivation and disbelieve in our own abilities, which again, originates from our fears. In most cases, we don't really want to do that "boring" task that we "have to" do to move forward with our agenda. Therefore, we beat around the bush, plan around it and seek for different tasks to do. We escape our purpose and start to convince ourselves that we have to clean our room, organize our photos or read another blog article. We lie to ourselves by giving extreme importance to very mundane tasks that can easily be scheduled ahead. Nevertheless, we want to do them now, because we know exactly how to bring them to success. In contrary to new and unknown ventures, they're easy to finish and we know exactly what to expect. They're guaranteed successes rewarding us with a fake sense of accomplishment. However, without realizing, we start to push away our inner-longings, because we're actually hiding from a confrontation with our own incompetence. We're simply avoiding what we know we sincerely have to do.

So, question yourself. "Is it really important to do that task I am going to do?" "Is it crucial to do it now?" "What is it that I have to do to bring me closer to my goal?" "What are the essential tasks I have for today?" "What is the biggest problem I have to conquer?" Commit to what you have to do. There is no other way.

Thereby, you will find that when you start doing what you're supposed to be doing, you're being much more satisfied. You can now prove yourself that you can overcome little challenges. They will feel as personal victories, because it demonstrates your abilities and potential. These positive confirmations reinforce your confidence and serve as powerful encouragements to continue. Naturally, this will be your fuel for the remaining tasks ahead and days to come. And when you keep at it consistently, you don't want to do anything else anymore. You suddenly don't want to prevaricate, because your goal-driven desire will shoot through the roof. After all, you have an important mission to accomplish.

Subsequently, if you're serious about your goal, it has to be your number one priority. If you catch yourself doing something else, you clearly show that it's not your highest priority at that moment. You have to come to that conclusion and change it when necessary. Only by giving precedence to it, you demonstrate full commitment and show what it truly means to you. Otherwise, if your goal is just a plan B or plan C, you will leave room for different possibilities to sneak-in. Unconsciously; this leads to putting in less effort, making little excuses or seeking for different things to do.

Consequently, your actions will always prove your level of trust and faith in achieving a particular result. They naturally demonstrate the amount of belief you have. If you don't really believe in what you're doing, you will most likely lose motivation and eventually start doing something else. However, by having true commitment and belief in the outcome, you will automatically show your faith by taking massive action in that direction.

That's why; show your determination by excluding any other outcomes than the one(s) you truly desire. Thereby, believe in what you're doing and keep your focus fully on it. Keep picturing the exact result in your mind. Then work towards it. By staying in that focused space, you naturally tend to block out distractions and excuses. It keeps you right on track. All it takes is a dedicated mindset.

Ultimately, it's important not to distract yourself and shift your focus away from your purpose. There's always an excuse to do something else instead. Rather, just start with the first small task of your project. Take one little step. This will help you break a mental barrier and motivates you to make the next move. Thereby, simply concentrate on each little problem that appears and try to solve it. Keep doing that and you will automatically reach your destination in the most optimal manner. Just do what you truthfully have to do.

CREATE YOUR OWN PATH TO SUCCESS

Now, to summarize the moral of this chapter, I'd like to share another story with you. We have to go back in the day to the early 2010's. It was at that time I set sail on a new course as a music producer. I decided to start a long-term collaboration with a friend I recently met. My friend and I agreed on the mission to release our material for a professional record label company. We dedicated ourselves to it and let the obstacles come as they came.

As little did I know that collaborating with a completely different personality, could contribute so much to my growth. For instance, during our collaboration, my melody-making skills started to improve. It slowly started to click how my feelings and music-theory knowledge could work together to produce amazing results. Without realizing, I learned my friend's way of thinking and being. It was fruitful, so I automatically adopted some of his mental strategies.

Furthermore, his song-building qualities were outstanding. He came up with creative ways of arranging the instruments and making impressive build-ups and progressions. When you're in company with such a creative person, you automatically pick up some of that talent. In a way, he became my mentor and I become his'.

This positive vibe gave drive and inspiration. We felt good about what we were doing and naturally wanted to work. We did whatever we could do to learn. We searched for tutorials, read production forums and experimented courageously in our application. We were consistently proactive in our approach, because we believed in our mission. We had a purpose for the right reasons and started to create our own path to success.

However, a few years later, life took a turn. Our growth started to decline. We were slowly getting stuck in our own little world of doing things. We both were getting too familiar with each other's strengths and weaknesses. Inevitably, we had built a little bubble around us in which we lived. It was hardly possible to escape that space. Thereby, we were making the same mistakes repeatedly. We kept using similar strategies and thought "May be this time they will work." The belief in our capabilities to find solutions started to fade away. This took a toll on our creativity and inspiration.

However, we kept on going and without even realizing, negative feelings started to occupy our minds. We became easily frustrated and annoyed. Nonetheless, we forcefully kept true to our goals. Despite our efforts, it just didn't work anymore. Our motivation had dropped and killed our inspiration. We were only going through the motions without having a real desire. No longer were we convinced or committed. Our reasons weren't right anymore. It felt as if we "had to" do it, instead of love to do it. If we wanted to get out of the hole we dug for ourselves, we needed change.

Then one day, it was enough. I called my friend and respectfully told him I wanted to stop our collaboration. I explained how I felt and asked how he felt. Clearly, we were in a fruitless position and he understood. We just had to go our own ways in order for us to grow again. And after one last goodbye, we both went off, finding our new paths to success.

While getting used to being a solo producer, the cloud of negativity slowly started to dissipate. Gradually, new ideas and desires started to occupy my mind. Although completely different from before, they were pointing towards a fresh direction. A direction that ultimately took me on a path to become the creator of a successful EDM platform and international best-selling author. My secret? None. Just a good old-fashioned mission with a desire to provide value to the world.

When you understand this story, you can see how the path to success develops itself based on our choices. The paths we walk is always non-linear and tightly connected to our feelings. Our feelings speak the truth and reflect themselves in everything we do. That's why, if we commit to a mission with love-based motives, we already have what it takes to get there. The "how" takes care of itself when the "why" comes from the right place.

Want to be successful? Stop looking for the "right" path. Discover yourself and the path will be handed to you. Just care what you set out to do and let the doing come from how you feel. Don't let the feeling come from your doing. Feel first and then do. Do what feels right and what you truly wish to experience. Be whom you need to be to get where you want to go. After all, we have to be a certain way to produce a particular result. Thereby, follow what works and ditch what doesn't. If you keep doing that, life has no choice but to take you on a journey of fulfillment.

Once you're completely fulfilled, does it really matter what the route has been? Moreover, do you think you could ever have predicted the path you took? The path will always enfold right before your eyes exactly as it should be. It couldn't be any different, because it merely represents your learning curve throughout history.

In the end, our fate is in our own hands. We have to choose it, execute it and create it. Thereby, our level of success directly reflects our current state of understanding. An understanding we can decide to improve, and by doing so, naturally forms our optimal path to excellence.

CHAPTER 4:

THE MINDSET OF SUCCESS

You now have all the ingredients to obtain the ultimate success mindset. You need a well-defined purpose, keep your motivation and stay on your path until the end. However, to reach your goals, stay inspired and remain on track, you will have to adopt a growth mindset on the way. A growth mindset is a mental attitude towards progress. Progress demands change in a more advantageous direction.

GROWTH MINDSET VS. FIXED MINDSET

You see, the growth mindset is an open-minded way of thinking that allows new information to come in. Furthermore, it's an attitude of being convinced that there's always more to learn. The willingness to learn challenges our current beliefs and understandings. Thereby, always seeking the solution in consistent self-improvement.

Most people however, choose to dismiss a growth mindset and adopt a fixed mindset. A fixed mindset is a mental shield that covers the risk of being confronted with incompetence. This is a scary thought, so our egos get in the way by thinking we don't have to learn anymore. We think we know it all, yet know very little. This gets us stuck and sets us up for poverty or mediocrity. After all, the only way to progress is to become more than who we currently are. If we shut that off, decay kicks in, taking us to a place of adversity, dissatisfaction and eventually depression.

Therefore, if we want to be successful, it's absolutely critical to adopt a growth mindset. We have to drop our egos and stay open to new information and new ways of doing things. If we can do that, we can start to put all the pieces of our roadmap together and slowly work ourselves up to total awesomeness.

HOW TO KNOW IF YOU HAVE A GROWTH MINDSET

But how do we differentiate a growth mindset from a fixed mindset? How do we know if our way of thinking holds us back?

In most cases, we've embraced both the growth and the fixed mindset, depending on the situation. However, the balance is usually shifted towards a more fixed lookout on life. If you want to find out the truth in this regard, simply look at your results right now. Are you happy with your results? Is your work fruitful? Are your methods working? How successful are you? How capable are you? How do you feel about everything so far? If you're like most people, you probably feel that you can do better. This is okay, but you have to realize that your current mindset has brought you to where you are today. If you are happy with that, then keep going in that direction. However, if you are not, then maybe it's time for change. Real change.

HOW TO CHANGE YOUR MINDSET

So, what if you want to do better? How do you go from a fixed mindset to a growth mindset?

First, realize that everything we perceive goes through our own filter of understanding. If our understanding is small, we can't process much new information. Learning is cumulative, so new information can only get through if it's at the level of our current knowledge base. If it goes beyond that, we mostly fail to absorb it. Thus, we're tempted to reject it so that we don't have to deal with it. This can keep us stuck in a small world of ignorance. However, if we want to break that, we consciously have to focus on any new information with an intent to figure it out. It's about our willingness to explore it, regardless of our current level of understanding. We have to start at our own level and learn from there. When we genuinely do that, we grow our awareness and slowly create a wider perspective. Hence, we go from narrow-minded to more broad-minded.

So, the solution is simple. Just make a conscious choice. Choose to change. Choose to do it different. Choose to stay open minded. It's just a matter of focusing on being different. Not just as a wish, but as a deeper genuine desire. You have to change your self-image by picturing a person who is more open, who wants to grow, who wants to learn, and who wants to understand. Thereby, you have to abandon the person who you think you are right now.

The person who you think you are right now has these limiting beliefs. He/she has adopted a self-defeating identity that masks the truth: being fearful. To escape reality, we think we have to present an image to the outside world. An image where we play the know-it-alls or put our heads in the sand. An image that requires us to shutoff learning and growth, because it may expose our weaknesses. We just don't want to risk being confronted with our lack of competence or the pain of not feeling loved. That's why we have to pay attention to our fears. They hold us back. They keep us down, yet they're not real. They're just negative predictions of our imagination.

Obviously, it's in our best interest to overcome our fears and change how we feel. We have to mature and outgrow them. How do we do that, you may ask? Simply have an intent to do it. Choose to be different. Choose to feel different. Choose to be someone else. Someone braver, someone better. Don't hold on, but let go. Don't resist, but surrender. What you resist persists and what you look at disappears. Nothing bad will happen when you choose to see it that way. Accept that you're going to fail and be okay with that. Accept that people are going to judge you and be okay with that too. Simply accept the worst, surrender to the consequences and it'll take the bite out of the fear. Decide that you're not going to feed into any negative emotions. Choose to stay in a stable emotional state, no matter what happens. Consciously move away from a chaotic feeling space into a calm feeling space.

Furthermore, it also helps to gain new experiences different from the ones you imagine. New experience can help you override any lies you believe are true. That is, if you're having a serious intent to do so. For example, if you're afraid in the dark, go for a nightly walk and make it a positive experience. Convince yourself it's going to be okay. This way, you collect first-hand evidence that your fear is nothing more than a powerless paper tiger.

Of course, it can take some time for a fear to dissipate. It typically will not go down without a fight, especially the bigger ones. Accept that and keep at it anyways. Think, "Bring it on!" You're in charge. Thereby, see it as an exciting challenge and not as a struggle or battle. Over time, they will fade away. Once they do, a weight falls off your shoulders and you will feel lighter and more confident. So, challenge yourself and each time you catch yourself going into a negative feeling space, use your will to move into a positive feeling space. All it takes is some consistent conscious focus and you will receive the benefits.

By overcoming our fears and changing our limiting self-beliefs, we allow ourselves to open up. It shifts us from a fixed mindset to a growth mindset. So, reinvent yourself. Change the negative thoughts into positive ones. Come from a place of curiosity and genuine interest. Drop the ego and do it different this time, because you said so.

HOW TO AVOID A FIXED MINDSET

Now, what does a fixed mindset and growth mindset look like in practice? What are some behavioral traits that show if, what and how we need to change?

One of the major indicators of a fixed mindset is the attitude of looking for an easy way out. The easy way out is a poor mentality where we want to exert as little effort as possible for the biggest gain possible. People with this attitude secretly want others to do the work for them. They want to be pampered, spoon-fed and swallow a magic pill. They *wish* an outcome to occur; but they don't truly *want* an outcome to occur. It's a lazy and passive demeanor, hoping that one day; their desires magically appear on their lap. However, they don't realize that they're responsible for their own fortune. Thus, they gravitate towards a victim mentality and point fingers to the outside world.

Clearly, this leads to pain, struggles, frustration and possibly desperation, as people can never seem to get what they want. The outside world is simply not the cause of their bad luck. We create our own luck. Therefore, the solution is easy. We have to stop looking at the outside world and focus more on the inside world. The problem doesn't lay in the outside, but in the inside. Our inside (who we are) will only reflect in the outside (what we do). Consequently, if our inside is mostly negative, we will get negative experiences. And vice versa, if our inside is mostly positive, we will get positive experiences. So, if we change ourselves, our new desires will manifest in the outside world. Why? Because who we are dictates what we do, including the benefits we reap.

That's why we need to drop this easy-way-out attitude and adopt a new one. We have to take responsibility and show the willingness to change ourselves, instead of waiting for others to give us what we want. We need to stop pampering ourselves and give away our personal power. We have to be proactive and figure things out on our own. Thereby, the level of engagement with our tasks indicates our eagerness to grow.

Quite often, I receive messages from people asking me to give them an easy-way-out solution. Even if I just gave them tremendous value in a tutorial video, they're still not satisfied. It's never enough. Either they want to have my creation for themselves or they seek an instant shortcut to a particular result. They want it now and they don't feel like going through the process. Whether we like it or not, high quality creations require (long) processes. By gracefully going through the process, we can actually fulfill our potential and become an outstanding music producer. The process is essential for success. After all, if we get better, our results get better.

So, ask yourself; are you sometimes looking for an easy way out? Are you expecting others to do the work for you? Are you sometimes too passive or lazy to take action? Are you seeking for magic pills, special tricks or instant shortcuts? If you are, chances are you've not yet adopted a mindset for growth. Obviously, your growth determines whether you will climb to the top of the mountain or stay in the valley behind. If you want to get to the top, be proactive, take initiative and open your mind. Desire to figure things out yourself and don't stop until you understand it deeply and thoroughly.

Another big indicator of a fixed mindset is the amount of pigheadedness someone shows. Pigheadedness is the poor mentality where we definitively think we're (always) right. When we think we're right, we instantly close the door for different perspectives and interpretations. We just don't want to see another way or explore a different truth. It's an inflexible way of being that presents itself in stubbornness and an unwillingness to change.

However, our willingness to change is crucial if we want to grow. By resisting that, we rob ourselves from the ability to move forward. It holds us back and keeps us stuck. That's why it's important to examine your level of pigheadedness in situations. Do you just want to talk about what you know or are you open to new input? Do you want to learn from feedback or reject it? Do you want to be the know-it-all or the life-long student? Do you seek to understand or to disregard? Do you prefer staying inside your bubble of ignorance or stepping outside? Come clear with your attitude and change it when necessary. Just move out the space of unreceptiveness and move into the space of receptivity. Catch yourself when you close down and focus on opening yourself up.

Now, don't confuse pigheadedness with stubbornness. Stubbornness can both be good and bad, depending where it comes from. If it originates from the desire to defend your ego, it's usually a bad thing. The ego just wants to hide the truth: you feel weak and vulnerable when your limited capabilities are being exposed. To deal with that, you remain stubborn and biased. You thereby hold on to old ideas and attach your identity to those. On the contrary, if stubbornness comes from the desire to seek a deeper understanding, it can be a good thing. Seeking a deeper understanding is important to grow. It's not so much that you want to be pigheaded; you just want to grasp and interpret a new idea. You want to know the truth, without having to adopt beliefs or vague assumptions. So, be stubborn in a good way and not in a bad way. Stay open-minded, but remain skeptical. Test and explore the boundaries of an idea to examine within which perspectives it's valuable.

Illustratively, when you own a public YouTube channel, you receive many comments. Most are very positive, which is awesome, but some show exactly the destructiveness of being pigheaded. For example, sometimes people question my less-is-more approach. They say something along the lines of "So and so says that you shouldn't use a brick-wall limiter on your track." Technical terms aside, I usually give them two answers. One, "Does it work?" Two, "Feel free to learn from so and so and see where it takes you." By them being narrow-minded, they condemn a different way of doing, which actually hurt their own growth. Completely unnecessarily, they close their own door, because they have adopted a limiting belief about how it should be.

No matter how you think it should be, the truth is always perspective-based. This means that there are many different ways to produce results, also depending on your outcome. It's never a matter of right and wrong. It's merely a matter of better or worse. So, find what works best for you by staying open to different approaches and thereby evaluate the results first-hand. If they're better, keep them. If they're not, let them go. Don't attach yourself to a particular method or certain viewpoint. Let it evolve.

Now, one last signal that indicates a fixed mindset is the low amount of self-esteem someone displays. As all negative feelings do, low self-esteem comes from fear. The fear makes us feel uncertain and unsure about ourselves. When we're uncertain and unsure, we doubt ourselves and don't like to move forward, because we're just being afraid of any consequences. We think we don't have the guts or skills to do what we have to. We worry, "What if things go wrong?" "What if I lose control?" or "What will people think?" So, we stick our heads in the sand and put an anchor to our souls.

On the other hand, having a low self-esteem can also result in compensation strategies. Compensation strategies are things we do to make up for how we really feel. We may compare ourselves to others to see if we are better than they are. We may seek people's approval to remove any responsibilities from our choices. We may even adopt a competitive mindset to keep proving to ourselves that we are the best. We will fall into the trap of a constant need for verification that we are indeed good enough. Yet, this thirst can never be quenched. There's always someone better and there's always more to prove.

Whether we put our heads in the sand or try to compensate for our incompetence, it's always an attack on our ability to grow. You see, we need to pull our heads out of the sand in order to listen. We have to throw ourselves out there and engage in stimulating activities to expand our horizon. Also, we need to stop compensating for our inabilities in order to learn from the best. We have to embrace our inexperience and seek to actualize new ideas.

That's why, don't walk away from change and don't feel the need to be better than someone else. That's just your lack of self-esteem. Life is not a competition or a consistency, rather a schoolhouse for us to grow. Accept it for what it is and work with it, not against it. After all, the only constant is change.

Accordingly, stop comparing yourself to others, but show your appreciation. Be inspired. Cheer for them and learn from them. Envy them, but don't be jealous. Feel motivated and encouraged by everyone. We all have different qualities and talents to offer.

HOW TO BE MORE CONFIDENT

Clearly, having a low self-esteem is not helpful, but where does it come from? Moreover, how can we improve our confidence?

Now, one of the reasons for a lower self-esteem is having unrealistic expectations. An unrealistic expectation is nothing more than an unattainable belief projected in the future. We assume something to become a certain way and attach our egos to that outcome. We get ahead of ourselves and celebrate prematurely. However, if it doesn't go as planned, we will be disappointed, frustrated and possibly discouraged. Thus, our self-esteem gets a beating, putting us further away from glory.

Again, the culprit in this regard is the quality of our choices. We choose for endeavors that are harmful for our self-esteem. However, they become our unhealthy habits and without realizing, stall our growth. For example, we connect on social media to these high-skilled masters that make us look like failures. We compare ourselves to fitness models, which destroys our self-image. We even fall for lies in desperation for promising benefits, yet never come close to replicating these results. We just desperately want life to be different by putting our hopes in the hands of luck and fantasies that are usually too good to be true.

That's why it's important to be aware of your own expectations. Question yourself. "What do I want to happen?" "What do I expect to happen?" "What do I assume is going to happen?" "What is the result going to be?" "How would I feel if I don't get that result?" "Do I desperately need something to happen or do I love to see something happen?" Make clear from which emotional space you're coming. If you're coming from fear, you *need* something to happen. Fear is a bad motivator and lead to disappointments. In contrary, if you're coming from love, you just *strive* for a positive outcome. Love is a good motivator and makes your well-being independent of a particular outcome. It releases your attachments and frees your mind. Whatever is going to happen, you will accept it and move on.

In line with unrealistic expectations, we also have the tendency to think that we know a lot and always have the truth in mind. However, in actuality we barely know anything. We will always be limited and are somewhat blindfolded to see everything reality has to offer. Yet, we can't see that. After all, everything we know is all there is. Thus, we have a cognitive bias. We mistakenly think our cognitive abilities are greater than they are. This is commonly referred to as the Dunning-Kruger effect.

For example, when you're being introduced to a new topic, e.g. FL Studio, your confidence quickly shoots to the roof. Excitedly, you can see the benefits and mistakenly think that you can make some impressive songs overnight. However, as time goes on, you slowly realize how challenging it is to be acceptably good at your new craft. Accordingly, your confidence drops. You feel less competent and you start to understand there's a lot that you have to learn. Obviously, this can be overwhelming and therefore is the point where most people give up. But not you. If you keep working at it and improve your skills, your confidence will slowly come back. Over time, once you reach a considerable degree of expertise, your confidence is deservedly high again, because you honestly went through the process. You now own it, which in the end, is true understanding.

Coincidentally, if you happen to start out with FL Studio and you want to feel confident using it, why don't you pick up the FL Studio Beginner's Guide? I've written this well-received guide to reveal all the essential basics you need to make songs fast. Yet, without any unnecessary "overcomplications". Just visit this link to get started: https://www.amazon.com/dp/B07D8JM9W9.

In any case, that's why it's important to be aware of the Dunning-Kruger effect. You will always experience this specific learning curve with any new material. It's exciting in the beginning and you quickly develop unrealistic expectations of your own capacities. Then, you will slowly get a reality check. Accept that. Don't fight it. Stick with it anyways, because you have the genuine desire to study it. Over time, you will reap the benefits. Your adequacy will grow, which will make you feel good about yourself. And rightfully so.

HOW TO AVOID UNREALISTIC EXPECTATIONS

Clearly, having unrealistic expectations is not helpful for your confidence. But what about realistic expectations? What are realistic expectations and how do we know if they're realistic or not?

In short, it's not helpful to have expectations at all. Realistic or not, any expectation will set you up for potential disappointment. There's no need for expectations. They don't serve you. Above all, it's part of a fixed mindset. You can only be happy with a highly specific result. It demands a one-sided outcome and dismisses any other possibilities. Instead, just focus on your mission and strive to do it good. Keep all your options open and let life surprise you. Simply, let it come to you and don't chase it. Attract, don't repel.

But how do we have an idea if something is realistic or not? How can we guestimate if something is helpful for us, even if we don't have any expectations?

Here's the trick: if something seems too good to be true, it usually is. As discussed earlier, there is no magic pill, especially when you pursue a bigger purpose. The magic pill is just a fantasy we use to escape our responsibilities and to hide a deeper fear. Thus, stay skeptical to anyone who promotes magic. Moreover, you want to look for independent social proof and real world application. If many different people gain real results, it may actually be worthwhile.

Most importantly, conduct your own research and try to understand it deeply. When you understand something deeply, you can clearly see what's true or not. You can see what works, what can potentially work and what's less likely to succeed. Thereby, don't make impulsive choices based on your fear's desires, but stay calm and give yourself some time to figure it out. No need to rush things.

In terms of music production, this means that you have to understand what it takes to get exceptionally good. It will be a long-term process with setbacks and breakthroughs. Be okay with that. See it as a challenge and keep your growth-rate open. You don't know how quickly you can progress. Nor can you see where you are in just a few months from now. However, if that scares you, may be you shouldn't have that aspiration right now. Find an outlet that works for you. One where you're willing to go all in. Nonetheless, if you really set your mind to it, you can change how you feel within a split second.

How to Understand Something Better

So, we want to learn something, but how can we accelerate our learning curve? Is there a way to gain a better understanding quickly? Additionally, how can we see through any surface value?

The key lesson to get a bigger understanding is to focus on the "why" and not so much on the "what" and "how". The "why" will immediately help you dig deeper and discover the true nature of things. For example, if a client asks you to dig a hole, you can apply the "what" and "how" to dig a perfect hole, which is very valuable. However, you have no idea what the purpose is. Why does the hole need to be there? What is its function? What is the outcome the client has in mind? What is the intent for his order? May be he wants to build a well for his community. Alternatively, maybe he wants to set a trap and take care of some unfinished business. This way, you have to think critically and use your common sense to look beyond the surface. More often than not, your common sense will tell if something is worth your time or not. Listen to how you feel and don't be afraid to ask any "why" questions.

Moreover, a good understanding of the "why" automatically generates the "what" and the "how" in most cases. To illustrate the power of knowing the "why", let's use an example. Imagine you're watching a tutorial where the teacher shows how to remove the lower frequencies from a lead sound. By only focusing on the "what" and "how" you can successfully copy his method and apply it yourself. You can model his exact settings and yield the same results. However, when you have to work on a different lead for a new song, you suddenly run into problems. You don't know what to do anymore or how exactly you should do it. Being clueless, you think "Do I have to remove the lower frequencies or not? If so, where and how much do they need to be removed?" This leaves you in the unknown, because you don't understand it well enough. After all, you've never focused on the "why".

You see, the "what" and the "how" can only teach you a trick or a commando. They don't let you think critically. You basically follow an order and that's it. You can change that by genuinely asking the "why". Why do you need to remove the lower frequencies of your lead sound? The "why" then produces a field of context in which the "what" and "how" exist. The answer could be; you have to remove the lower frequencies, because the kick and the bass will fill up that area. If the lower frequencies of these sounds collide, they will cause your mix to rumble and eat up a big chunk of the volume headroom. "Wow! I get it!" you excitingly think. It finally clicked. You gained a deeper understanding and found the reasons for doing your tasks. Now you're not dependent anymore on using a simple trick, but you can rely on your personal understanding.

This way, the better your understanding, the easier you can reproduce results within different situations. As far as this example goes, you can now predict how to remove the lower frequencies of any type of lead. You can just look at the frequency spectrum the kick and bass occupy and use that as your reference. So, if they occupy until around 130 Hz, you know immediately how to modify your lead, without having someone to tell you that. That's why; always ask for the "why". The "why" is the highway to growth.

Besides, by growing your understanding, you will also develop your own working strategies. You will find that you start doing things in your own ways. Not because you "have to" but because you "want to". This is a good sign and indicates progress. It demonstrates authentic experience and early stages of mastership.

YOU'RE DOING TOO MUCH

So, what does this leave us with? How can we implement these ideas now? Where do we start?

Surprisingly, you don't have to do much. It's not about *doing* something. It's about *being* someone. Simply be someone with a growth mindset. Stop seeing yourself as having these unnecessary limitations. Just see yourself as having a winning mentality. Then, the "doing" will naturally rollout the character you choose to be. In a practical sense, this means to move forward and look at what you can do right now by being someone you desire. It is in the now where you make your choices. Only in the now you can demonstrate who you truly are and what you are made of.

To understand the power of being someone, let's ask a couple of questions. What do you have in mind when you want to win a game of soccer? Do you picture yourself as Mr. Clumsiness or Cristiano Ronaldo? Of course, Cristiano Ronaldo! Similarly, what do you have in mind when you want to be successful asking a crush out on a date? Do you picture yourself as Mr. Nobody or James Bond? Of course, James Bond! Did Cristiano Ronaldo and James Bond never made a mistake? Of course not. Yet, by imagining you being them, you automatically ask yourself "What would this person do in this situation?" and "How should I feel to be like him?" By stepping into the shoes of an ideal character, you seek to model his/her successful state of being. You want to gain a "feel" for being in a profitable mindset.

You see, you simply need to get in a certain optimal state to get the results you're looking for. That optimal being state can be referred to as "love". Love is what feels right (not necessarily what feels good). It's a fearless calm attitude that shows complete trust in your own capabilities and potential, even when that means you're just a beginner. This is called confidence (not to be confused with arrogance, which originates from fear). With a high level of confidence, you're not that worried. No matter what happens, you will deal with it and find a way. You simply have faith, trust and a positive outlook on whatever life throws at you.

Accordingly, our best projects will always be the ones where we think highly of ourselves. That is, in a convictional confident manner. That's why you have to practice assigning high-quality identities to yourself and being convinced they're true. The cliché I-can-do-it mindset. This will put you in an optimal motivated learning state. At the same time, ditch the ones that hold you back. You have to reprogram yourself as being a high-value individual with infinite potential to bring any task to success. Then, just go do it. Therefore, if you believe you can, then you can indeed. Similarly, if you believe you can't, then you can't indeed. Thus, be careful what you believe in.

CHAPTER 5:

EXPERIENCE SUCCESS

As you probably understand, any successful undertaking requires experience. However, experience itself is not enough. It's not just about going through the motions. It's all about using the experience to improve yourself. The experience serves as a feedback platform to develop your abilities and understanding. Thereby, you need to practice new methods, train yourself to be a certain way and rehearse your execution. As they say, repetition is the mother of all skills and practice makes perfect.

Going through repetition enables you to remember who you have to be to produce a desired outcome. By remembering who you are in that situation, you instantly recognize what a positive result should look like, sound like or feel like. It creates this deeper intuitive connection, which ultimately defines the quality of your state of being.

Therefore, you have to learn to get in a state of flow and become one with your instrument or vehicle. Thereby, be present in the moment. For instance, an incredible racecar driver is not just driving his car. He doesn't think what to do or how to do it anymore. It comes naturally to him. He simply becomes one with the car. He is the car. He has to be to perform at his best. Else, if he starts thinking, judging and analyzing he snaps himself out of his flow, which leads to making mistakes. To prevent that, he goes into the mental state where he blindly relies on who he truly is: an incredible racecar driver. Similarly, an amazing pianist becomes one with the piano. He doesn't think how to play the piano. He is the piano. Likewise, a fantastic soccer player becomes one with the ball. He doesn't think how to play the ball. He is the ball.

Naturally, masters make their choices based on what feels right in the moment. They intuitively feel their way to perfection. Obviously, they didn't reach a high level of mastery overnight. They simply put in the time with a deeper desire to improve their abilities. Gradually, their practice sunk in to a deeper level and became part of who they are.

Hence, if you want to be good at something, you have to exercise important tasks. Keep repeating them with an intent to do it better. Learn, implement and improve. Consistently repeat the process and do it (slightly) different each time. Explore new potential ways and experiment. And once you've found a better way, go over at it one more time. Thereby, feel what it's like to be successful. Feel what it's like to be in an optimal state of mastery. Live it to become it. Make it part of who you are. Not just intellectually, but let it sink in to an intuitive level. Inevitably, this requires practice, direct experience and your willingness to do it.

This holds true for this book as well. Are the messages presented herein important to you? Are the strategies valuable for your growth? Are you dedicated to implement these ideas? Because if you are, you already know what to do. Read it again, apply and practice. Let it sink in and try to understand it deeply. Naturally, this is what you're going to do, because you are committed to fulfill your highest potential. Once you start fulfilling your highest potential, success will come to you and you will never run without. You will experience it in abundance, because you're the one creating it.

Success is just a matter of choice. The choice is yours. Make it count.

WHERE TO GO FROM HERE

You've already had your first success by reaching the end of this book. Awesome! Although I didn't have any doubt in my mind you wouldn't, it's still very much respected. You simply showed your determination and commitment by following through. Additionally, you showed a high level of trust and faith in my work. Thank you for that. It means a lot to me.

Now, since you're at the end, where do you have to go from here? Obviously, the choice is yours. However, may be you'd like to learn more from me. If you do, why don't you come and take a look what *Screech House* has to offer for you? You will find valuable music-making strategies that I share with like-minded people across the globe. You can join now by visiting the links below.

Website: https://screechhouse.com
YouTube: https://youtube.com/screechhouse
Books: https://amazon.com/author/screechhouse

Love to see you there, but don't forget to bring your growth mindset.

- Cep
(Music producer, author & creator of *Screech House*)

GET YOUR FREE SAMPLE PACK

To help you kickstart your music productions, I've created a free hardstyle sample pack (EDM samples included) to share with you. If you're into making EDM, feel free to download your copy by visiting the link below.

http://eepurl.com/cYAah1

ABOUT THE AUTHOR

Cep from *Screech House*, a high-skilled Dutch EDM producer, CEO and international best-selling author.

Cep is single-handedly responsible for the success of thousands of producers worldwide. They finally had their breakthrough by using Cep's notorious, but exclusive "less is more" strategies.

Cep's rise to success did not come easily. The amount of time and energy he had to put in is unheard of. This came with inevitable consequences...

Most people didn't understand Cep's career path and quietly gave up on him. Without any support, he had to deal with all the struggles and frustration that comes with becoming a professional artist. This almost led him to give up his dreams on many occasions.

But there was something inside of Cep that kept him going. Locked away inside a tiny room he had one mission and one mission only: being the absolute best in creating exceptional high-quality songs on a simple computer. He just had to succeed. And that's exactly what he did.

But once his music far surpassed that desired professional level, Cep wanted to quit. For good. He felt that it wasn't his calling in life anymore. He felt a much bigger calling was waiting: giving people the lifetime opportunity to replicate his success.

After more than a decade, he worked himself into the position to show everybody how to get the same results. He feels responsible for sharing the truth and giving people ultimate shortcuts in making their own music. This gave birth to *Screech House*, the definitive platform for making electronic dance music, mainly in FL Studio.

Cep wants to show you how to keep it simple and still yield incredible professional results. He strongly believes in removing the fancy tools or equipment and only focusing on the essential basics. This means that, when you discover his techniques, you will understand that high-quality music always follows the same proven tricks and secrets.

Now, Cep's work isn't just for everyone. He advocates that only dedicated producers will ever get to the top. That's why he has a big preference of only sharing his work with highly committed people. They need to have a learning mindset.

If you think you have the learning mindset, Cep's books are must-reads. They offer you to do less work, yet get much better results. How is this possible, you may ask? Simple. You don't understand the essential music-making basics well enough yet. Because if you do, creating a professional song becomes a walk in the park.

Get free access to Cep's work by visiting the *Screech House* website:
https://screechhouse.com

Follow Cep on the *Screech House* YouTube channel:
https://youtube.com/screechhouse

Obtain all Cep's books by going to the *Screech House* author page:
https://amazon.com/author/screechhouse

Printed in Great Britain
by Amazon